For Carol,

GREEN JOURNEY

RED BIRD

*Thank you so much
for your inspiration
and the wonderful
work in this book
and outside it.*

Poems by

Mary Kay Rummel

*Love & I wish
you wonderful years.
Mary Kay*

Loonfeather Press
Bemidji, Minnesota

Cover art "Borrowed Scenery" by Carol Struve
First printing 2001
Printed in Canada
ISBN 0-926147-13-7

Green Journey, Red Bird was made possible, in part, by a grant
from the Region 2 Arts Council through funding from the
Minnesota State Legislature

Loonfeather Press
P.O. Box 1212
Bemidji, MN 56619

*This book is dedicated to
Tim, Timothy, and Andrew*

*the memory of my father,
William Simpson*

*the memory of my mother,
Mary Woulfe Simpson*

ACKNOWLEDGMENTS

Grateful acknowledgment is made to the editors of the following journals in which these poems first appeared:

100 Words: "Camouflage," "Reading the River"
Alaska Quarterly Review: "Advent"
Bloomsbury Review: "Crocheting"
California Quarterly: "Going In"
Comstock Review: "Those Who Sing"
Earth's Daughters: "Northern Women"
George Washington Review: "No Straight Lines"
Hawaii Pacific Review: "Her Hoof, Her Black Muzzle"
Language Arts: "What Is a Place But a Story"
Loonfeather: "A Stone Womb at Solstice," "Boatyard Late October," "Finding the Jungfrau"
Luna: "That and Not," "Family Stories"
Mankato Review: "To the Wild"
Minnesota Poetry Calendar: "In the Shore Drift," As if the Solstice in Kilarney," "Tall Birds Stalking"
Mythos: "And the Dead Shall Speak"
Nimrod: "Tongues of Women/Tongues of Angels," "Birches"
Northeast: "Without Her, Nothing," "Beneath Me, Behind Me"
Passages North: "Neither Bones Nor Wings"
Rag Mag: "River Tongues"
Sidewalks: "At the Side Altars," "Letter From the Middle," "Her Winter Heart," "Moorings," "Symbiosis"
Sing Heavenly Muse: "A Story She Wraps Around Herself"
Thirty-Three Minnesota Poets. Ed. Monica and Emilio DeGrazia. "Reading," "A Medieval Herbal." Minneapolis: Nodin Press; 2000
The McGuffin: "Choose Me, Father"
Water-Stone: "A Medieval Herbal," "Symbiosis"
"Birches," "River Tongues," "At the Side Altars," "A Story She Wraps Around Herself," and "What Can a Woman Take" appear in the limited edition chapbook, *The Long Journey Into North* published by Juniper Press.

Thank you to Betty Rossi, Gail Rixen and Penelope Swan of Loon-feather Press for their support.

Thanks also to Patricia Barone and Monica Ochtrup for reading the work in this manuscript in advance of publication. Thanks to Sharon Chmielarz, Carol Masters, Kate Dayton, Barbara Sperber, Nancy Raeburn and other Onionskin members for their help with these poems over the years.

I am grateful to the Vermont Studio Center and Norcroft Foundation for the gifts of time and space which helped me complete this book.

CONTENTS

I. A WOMAN'S TONGUE   3
What Tongue to Use

What She Thinks She Sees   4
River Tongues   6
A Little Helper   7
At the Side Altars   8
A Story She Wraps Around Herself   10
And the Dead Shall Speak   12
Birches   15
Tongues of Women/Tongues of Angels   16
Shore Drift   17
The Space Between   18
Northern Women   19
How To Do The Ropes Course   20
To the Wild   23
On the Celtic Fringe   24
A Medieval Herbal   25
What Is a Place But a Story   27
Reading   28
A Stone Womb at Solstice   29

II. I CANNOT LIVE IN MY OWN LAND   31
As if the Solstice in Kilarney

Graffiti on the Pier   32
Crocheting   33
Flesh and Wood   34
A Boat Called Coffin Ship   35

The Ancient Order of Hibernians 38

Reading the River 39

No Straight Lines 40

Whose Hands Are These 41

Choose Me, Father 43

Without Her, Nothing 44

Boatyard, Late October 46

Storyteller 47

III. HAUNTED BY THE THROBBING AND 48
  THE WAY IT SHAPES TIME

IV. NEW HOMES, NEW PLACES TO DIE 55
  Beneath Me, Behind Me

Sing 56

Her Hoof, Her Black Muzzle 57

Paper Landscape 58

Ceremony of Water 59

That and Not 60

Letter From the Middle 62

Her Winter Heart 63

Going In 65

Advent 66

Neither Bones Nor Wings 67

Camouflage 68

Eye Cantos 69

Symbiosis 71

At the Blues Saloon 72

Finding the Jungfrau 74

What can a woman take 76

Melody for a Long Marriage   77
Naming Them   78
Moorings   80
After My Father's Death   81
Tall Birds Stalking   82
Red Bird In Winter   83

Illustrations

Gardens by the Sea, 3
Fragment, 14
North to South, 21
River Tree, 39
Spring Storm Watch, 49
Back Forty, 52
Black Water, Orange Tree, 62
Northland Winter Journey, 63

GREEN JOURNEY

RED BIRD

I

A WOMAN'S TONGUE

What Tongue to Use

My language is made of water
tongues of rain, that demure
leveler, cloud-sent plain maker
of the twisted swollen green
hungry sea tongues
hissing, swallowing
the apples cut by horses' hooves on the beach
where the past disappears in seconds

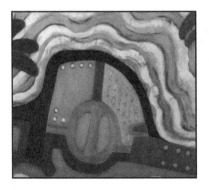

What She Thinks She Sees

The smell of fresh tar brings back the steaming kitchen
her mother angry about dirty shoes, that shining goo
irresistible as Brer Rabbit's magic tar baby.

The truck lumbering past the small houses, spraying tar
from its underside left a feeling of being marooned
surrounded by impassable streets.

The ice man came most summer days. With forceps
he hauled the block to the ice box her job
to empty the fast-filling pan beneath.

A horse clapped by once a week pulling a wagon with driver
calling, "Rags to buy, rags to sell." She thought that street
was her soul but it's become a freeway.

Is her soul another place she must find her way to? Her father's
soul is St. Paul, she knows and his grandfather
left his spirit in Galway.

Sometimes she thinks she sees her soul in those photographs
of night that are of light, the red maple leaf turning
on black water after sunset

In long brushes of deep violet, flood indigo, lime brilliance?
In the obsessive cardinal's song, ink-tongued cry, we live
we live, we live everywhere.

or in the line of arctic hares pink with a sun already gone,
shining garden lanterns strung out across the ice crust

or the island almost but not closing the way to the larger
lake might be the shape of her soul. In the heart
of not having where can she search?

River Tongues

My brothers claimed the river, last wilderness in old St. Paul,
their tongues, Mississippi tongues, their treasures, river-given
pelt   rabbit   rock.
Each summer day they slammed the screen door on their way,
fishing poles bobbing like antennas on their bikes.

"Stay away from the river," my mother warned. "It's
dangerous."
Her vague words relentless as the Schmidt's sign that flashed
from the brewery I passed on my way to school.
I clung to the sidewalk even though the river caves called—

cool tunnels to the earth altar the boys named
Frankenstein's Bed. The dark church was the only place
I could go to dream of beauty and danger, a wildness
beneath the side altars where Mary and Joseph

rising from their own stories said, *be holy, silent, ordinary
as clover*, like Mrs. Carlone's scarved head touching the front
pew.
Mary's statue smiled at a girl I knew, never at me.
I squinted but her alabaster remained serious and absolute.

A Little Helper

That's what my mother wanted.
It was hot work. She wore print dresses
and told me to iron while my brothers ran
to the river with BB guns and hunting knives.
Their shirts, rolled like sausages, waited, damp
until the iron flattened them.

One week of shirts for five men,
iron, brick heavy, sprinkle
the water bottle, slap it down,
push steam ahead of it, travel
those wide cotton backs,
do the yokes without wrinkling,
the narrow sleeves.

The day her brother, Patrick, fell at work
Mother asked me to iron while she waited
at his bed. I dug through the pile for
the easiest shirts, then ran to the beach.

When her brother died
I drowned in her rage

over the ironing undone, the daughter
who was never a help, or helper, over
our unspoken loneliness as my brothers
slammed the door on their way in and out again.

At the Side Altars

Instead of the mother
we were given the son
bleeding over and over—

Be like him
Die everyday to yourself
Be like him they said,

But reading each woman saint

We were given
our souls:

Therese in her French convent

knew hell on a pin head
all the love she carried for god
ripened as a rose in her,
lips parted in song
as his language sunk in.
Her suffering made her sing.

Rose of Lima

lived in silence
was cut by a surgeon
without anodyne
never cried
wore a crown of twisted
metal under her veil
never spoke about the killing
in the Peruvian hills.

Italian Maria Goretti

was murdered
while fighting a rape
she forgave Allesandro
as he stabbed her
he in prison felt remorse
she of course wasn't there to see it.
A model for us the nuns said.

I tried to be like them
a saint of West Seventh.
Went to the dentist
who didn't use novocaine.
For three hours on Good Friday
imagined myself into a frenzy
like the best of penitentes
then skipped out in relief.

> *My saint now is the Roman Barbara*
> *who broke silence*
> *her head kept talking*
> *as it rolled away from her body.*

A Story She Wraps Around Herself

The boot marks of the unfortunate are to be seen on the gray stones of the beach.   Peig Sayers

Here on Clougerhead waves crash
on granite cliffs, steaming shafts
of rock shatter the Atlantic.

Three miles out the deserted green hills
of the Blasket Islands mourn the lost
civilization of the tongue.

I imagine your black skirt slicing through wind,
your rosary dangling from your large red hands.
It was this sea that gave you stories
for your neighbors and later for the scholars
who came to hear your words, foreign to their ears.

You carried your dead son from the cliff bottom.
With unshaking hands you rearranged his skull
for burial. Once, you allowed yourself to cry
then clapped the end of mourning, found the words to pray.

And you made the men pray, those who came to listen.
Made them kneel on the cold flagstone.
They had to say the rosary with you,
the Angelus, blessings for sick and non-sick,
for sinners and non-sinners
and you kept them at it as long as you could.

You talked with your hands as well as your tongue,
a clap of the palms for urgency
a flash of thumb over your shoulders
your hand over your mouth to show a secret.

It's hard to be growing old you said
but I'll be talking after my death.
A woman's tongue is a thing
that doesn't rust.

And the Dead Shall Speak

In the crypt of St. Michan's Church
in Dublin lie bodies uncovered
and perfectly preserved for centuries.
One of them is a crusader knight;
another is a nun.

His words:

They would put her in here, of all possible bones,
hers, to be preserved with mine.
She lies with her hands covering her groin
even now with nothing left to hide
and whatever was there to hide?

I traveled with Godfrey on a heavy horse
across the Hungarian plain.
Was mauled by a bear in Turkey.
Droves of Assyrians attacked us
and we huddled like sheep before
we won and built the castle on the coast.

I lost my hand scaling Jerusalem's wall.
Even when we stormed through Herod's Gate
into the Holy City, I didn't feel the way I felt
when I saw her so full of light throwing her
laughter to the sunless air.

She ran from me when all I wanted
was to show her the slow connection
our bodies could make. Into a convent she ran.
I brought the seeds of wild pinks from Jerusalem for her.
Scattered them among the graves.

Her words:

I was a virgin but that doesn't matter now.
All that saved flesh gone.
They told me I was wed to a god.
It was a cold union. Sometimes I dreamt
of that body on the cross, imagined it whole.

The old ones said I wanted men to notice me
and I did some days, even the wretched ones
who carried our grain in from the fields.
Evenings their eyes saw beneath the serge I wore
and I remembered the bodies of my brothers.

There was little pleasure even in summer.
Inside the walls our faces, crumpled white rags
atop arthritic bodies, twisted in perpetual winter.
Feast days the old ones ate meat.

My family threw me in here with the knight.
I died in plague time glad I had no children to lose.
Dead, my eyes filled with shadows of women
who came to our gates arms weighed down
with the bones of their children.

My flesh fell off but my bones stay
strong in death as they never were in life.
My head is still bowed as was customary.
I lie with the knight in the silence of our beginning,
all our costumes gone. Through the damp black
centuries our bones touch, sparks with no heat.
His are ramrod straight. I want to climb them.

My words:

I am the one who when I was young would
have thought of dying looking at these bones.
But here I am thinking of my life—no nuns in it at last.

I am the one whose body remembers a man.
I love his bones. My legs stretch wide to wrap him,
No nun but a Molly Bloom now and now and now.

Birches

They remind me of walking young
and alone through the cloister door
down the long tiled aisle in white,
then at the altar—the pull of my hair being cut.

I thought I had married god
holding nothing but air in my thin arms.
On hands and knees, my mouth pressed
to the floor, I felt invisible.

Years ago I walked out the heavy locked door
but the cloister followed me or I followed
the quiet hallways until it seems

that I've come back with arms held wide
but empty still. The first time was practice
for this season when women become invisible.

Men's eyes look through me now
as April morning sunlight slides down the length
of eastward facing trunks,
half of them wedded to light, half still in shadow,

like the egrets I saw last autumn, their bodies
punctuating a black pond, their reflections rooted
as if stillness were their one desire.

Tongues of Women/Tongues of Angels

Beneath the brush a hawthorne trails a knot of berries
from stubborn soil, a perfectly formed resilience.
A heron, stilted with head inclined, stands frozen
eyes intent, as blackbirds feed among the stones.

There's nothing gentle in this night bird that brings silence
to the pond, that stops the laughing red-wings,
jay's ululations, sputterings of sparrows, brings silences
from rocky shores all worn in her deep shimmer.

She turns her back to me, disappears in her white gown, her
nun's veil. Old one, round shouldered at prayer, lifts her wings
stares into tree visions, moves on in a blue shuffle.

All my life I have known these old women at prayer.
Crone dreams I never wanted live in an oak outside my door.
I've heard their shadows whisper, voices I collect with care
like charms I use to trade one darkness for another.

Shore Drift

This morning you want me to stay
in bed but you join me instead.
On the beach we watch the heron feed.
Is it not the same hungry eye
fast plunge, eating?

Let her show us
how to wait
how not to blink
away the light
and before dark
how to feed.
Let her teach us
both stillness
and the focused pounce.

Let beak let snake tongue
spit out winter reeds.
Let the juicy crab of summer
be plucked from mud
and swallowed whole.
Follow the trail of fish
in the throat all of it
stretching the skin sideways.

Ocean inside us outside us
licking and cleaning.
A distant plane hums
as heron skims waves
her body its sound.

The Space Between

All afternoon we sit on the beach.
Our talk, small: *child bread book*
words transparent and vulnerable.
The whole afternoon blooming protected
like the scarlet center of kale
and our speech its nourishing stem.
You create gentle endings for yourself.
I build middles and they are all beginnings
as if we could dream away one another's
past with our voices. Friends, our bodies
stretch while surf runs through sluices of sand.
Love idles, half asleep in the space between us.

Northern Women

Mid-May and trees bare, still.

From the radio a Newfoundland story,
a young moose chased by dogs onto ice
which became a floe taking her out to sea.

Where I live the harbor's ice-locked
though each day the melt takes more.

The moose still has a life to live.
A helicopter slipped a harness over her
and she rose, no, was taken, into air
like the Virgin in Giotto's Assumption
being lifted under the arms by angels.

Not like the old woman in Arctic stories
put on the floe to die where the wolves
can't get her. Her open eyes eat harshness
while she imagines the yellow eyes
of tundra forget-me-nots that cling to soil
made of those who came before. Until
the water takes her, she lives
                    on her own fat.

How To Do the Ropes Course

1 Look Up

From here everything flows downward.

Some of us change our lives
like this
one downward step
then another
until we stand in a new landscape
disoriented, bemused, all senses open
to the roar of it.

This rising that we love
then falling
takes us to the end.
The body starts to dry.
The moment of greatest pleasure
becomes movement without sound,
watching dancers from a distance.

2 Put on the Harness

You are gone
like a word I have
but can't find
name for a flower
drifting note
smear of appleskin
empty chair.

Later as I walk into the room
looking for something that I lost
the gladiola waves like a blue flag

and you are waiting.
Old friend, you say,
why did you worry?

**3 Put One Foot in Front of the Other
on the Balance Beam in the Trees**

It is like the time we lay
in the grass below stars, listening.
The adagietto was a wall
or a blue doorway in the wall
the long road into the north,
fire road that climbs between pines
then drops into silence behind silence
making us afraid.

The shadows behind trees becoming
x-rays of trees, your hands—
I remember stars
and your hands behind them.

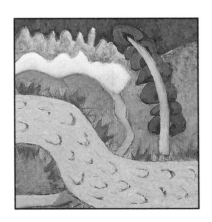

4 Jump Far from What We Are Losing

Most people stand on the platform
and leap. I sit on the edge
and squirm off feeling the wood
grind beneath me.

When we walked along the sand
your body had the feel of a running horse.
Now you leave like water leaves
the memory of debris on the shore.

You say there are no more seasons
for you. Something in you wants
to know the truth about the world
you say, meaning truth won't be
good when it's found.

Check harness. Close eyes. Push.
Between us the air, jagged.

To the Wild

I saw her once
as I skied the high country.
Two yellow points of light
measured me from a cave.
She had just moved
so the cubs could slide out.
One was already nuzzling
beneath her. I froze
then backed so slowly
into the way I'd come.

These winters
as I grow older
it seems that some exchange
transpired when our eyes locked.
My spirit feels trapped
in a heavy body
hiding when wind
torments the trees, snaps
the brown reeds.
It longs for one single
green growing thing.

Slow and easy I say
shambolic woman.
Listen to the wildness
growling
within you.

One morning
the bull of a sun
will summon you.
Or the smell of light
massaging the north face
of a tree.

On the Celtic Fringe

for Declan

Why do I return
to this place of stone? Declan Collinge

Stone to the sky
Stone to the sea
Stone spills
from windows in the hut.
Wild flowers widen every crack.
Connemaran country.

You named the flowers for me
as we walked the narrow road
between walls of stone and wild fuschia
cinquefoil suns, moons of meadowsweet
to the beach where our feet crushed
thick bulbs of bladder verach.

We told how the priests
taught us fear, how we changed
in the sixties, how music
and poetry saved us.

I picked up a rock curved to fit my fist
connemara marble, green and white
a frieze-like head of a woman protruding
shedding its slate as the moon its night.

Wider and wider her mouth opened.

A Medieval Herbal

Let he man drink out of a church bell
Yarrow   lupine   lichen   betony
Let him sing shile he drinks

Beati Immaculati

Let the woman remain a virgin
Until twenty-seven or -eight
Thus she will find her true origin

Let her drink fennel against folly

In her thirties when she is dry
She should climb the Tor of St. Catherine
Pick purple monkshood, beware the poison
In the root, but taste true passion

For heartache give brambles
Pound the leaves, lay them over the breast
Of both male and female

At forty she will explode with pleasure
Give her wild marjoram for a sore head
The spirit plant parsley in good measure

For the lunatic gentian and fennel

The herb of greatest future is marigold
If it be put in a church where the woman sits
Who has broken her matrimony
It will not let her leave until desire is put away

This has been proven true

At fifty the body will quiet
But she is not ready to stop
Rosemary cures impotence
For men and women both

Blessed be carnations for they
Shall be called the flowers of god
Grow pansies, love's casualty

Spider webs brush against her face
After rain she notices the fuzziness
Of late summer leaves
Finds it on her own skin
The hairs catch water, hold it
Now she is like rue

Rain and sun reach all of her

What Is a Place But a Story

happening over and over again?
Here? *Women are lost.*
Here? *Man fights bear.*
Here? *Great fish leaps.*
Here we say is *dead man's point.*

Now is our time for travel.
We name the stories as we stop
or pass them by.
This is the beach where labor pains began.
By the swamp we fought, said it was over.
On this peak we loved.

This is the place to watch whales breech
or for them to watch us.
Islands rise from mysteriously wealthy mist.
This water is post-orgasmic.
It waves crooked salmon fingers.
There is no ending.

Reading

There was a sound of geese from the bay
of geese or a harmonica
and the way the sun idled
over the lake's cloud wall
revealing hills burning
was the way the geese advanced
dragging their phrases
across the water not on wind
but on memory
and that is why white rabbits
startled from their daytime places
beneath bushes and under cars
resembled the words in a child's book
lessons divulged, lessons concealed.
For the child a word succumbs
one word that emerges apart from its fellows
to unroll its bright syllables everywhere
an urgent repetition that beats doubt away
word electricity that lights the dark.

A Stone Womb at Solstice

At Newgrange in Ireland is a megalithic burial chamber built over 5,000 years ago. In it, the curving loops of the great spiral show the journey of the soul, moving through death to rest and, at the solstice, rebirth in the central chamber.

1

We walk through the narrow passage.
              Curving spirals
carved in stone guide us
              to the chamber.
Stone spiral opens outward,
              moves downward,
womb with a window
              slit for the sun
at solstice.
On a ledge inside barn swallows
              build mud nests.
They dart and scold
              at our faces,
protect their chirping fledglings.

2

What is new is old.
Wild trajectories of birds
interlace egg-like stones.

Today I need to know
that death is birth.
I touch this cold text
with blind fingers
feeling for my story.

3

Ashes in the bowls of stone
witness the drive for birth.
Oracles from a time when women

never lived beyond mothering.
At home my sons grow distant
as the winter sun. Their hands
release mine.

The curving loops
of the great spiral
tell me to mother
my own life:

desire whose shape is
lost in the season of ice,
ice that has seized
the little bird's wing
song of bitter edge

Let the old chants in.
If there is light
let it be in me.

II

I CANNOT LIVE IN MY OWN LAND

As if the solstice in Kilarney

As if the sun rising this morning is pale moon

As if trees try to catch her light when it appears
through breaks like the slits cut in passage graves
saying *Here now, we'll hold you*

She moves on, an old woman beneath her layers
resting now, climbing now and we cannot see her

like my grandmother that jolly Kerrywoman
whom we did not know beneath her floured hands

As if I could become an opening for her light

Graffiti on the Pier: Dun Laoghaire

Fuck Immigration
Stay and Fight!

We carry the legacy
of that leaving.
A black hunger keeps
my family traveling.

When we're away we want to be home.
When we're home we want to be away.
We leave for homes that are not ours
look for blessings that we don't expect.

The oldest waited to marry until the parents died.
The others left the country. Priests walked the roads
keeping men on one side, women on the other.
There was no land. No food without land.
No sex without land. No love without sex.
The priests sent our parents to church.

The last chance whine
of the cicada drones

It's here and it's not ours
It's here and it's not ours.

Crocheting

At six in the morning we drive into Clare
the wind and the light working off each other
ocean wild with foam and glitter.
The rock a slate gray lake around us
and stone fences called lace, moon
sinking, still visible through their holes.

Aunt Catherine tells how our grandmother, Mary
half Flahivey, half Boucher, who feared
the sea and married a Limerick Woulfe,
sewed a hem by hand the night before she died.
Like the mother she learned from, she made lace
delicate as sea spray, strong as a stone wall.
I see her gloating over a fine feast of it.

When I was a nun, she knitted a shawl
for me, black and large as a table top.
The snow made lace on it the day I walked
crying, unable to attend her funeral.
You have to make your own pattern.
Don't just fill one out, she told me and tells me.

Each choice a needle flash, possible, gone.
On the water wild swans cut arcs of light.

Flesh and Wood

On my grandmother's birth certificate, below
the father's typed Thomas, his sign X
standing lonely on two legs tells
of Bromore birth in1880, well
rounded year, in Ballylongford
his wife, Johanna, his mark
a subjunctive that flies
west, wings shredded
hungry, wanting more.
Grandmother, Mary, under
her father's sign named, raised
my mother who loved to read, raised
me who loves to write. Across time
the X flashes a coda of stone, sea, boat,
bird to another rosetta story, a key, sliced
hourglass, code cracked, a xeroxed confidence,
the corners birch makes when it falls across pine

such a mot of swayings fatherly.

A Boat Called Coffin Ship

1

This is the shore you walked
the moonlight broken, then mending.
You, loving the sink of your feet
in sand, the grip of it, wanted

to stay on the edge of the sea
that gave, that took. You never swam
because you'd knitted the sweaters
that hung from the bones of your uncles
when they were pulled from the Atlantic.

I see your dark hair, your blue eyes
squinting at the glare as the boat
shoves off the trembling pier.

You left Ireland's hunger
in a slaves' coffin ship,
prayed rosaries during wild storms
sure that you would die.

2

From the shanty towns of Boston you
moved far from the sea as you could.
Never longed for the grit of salt.
Never heard the cries of seabirds.
Never let your children in a boat,
or taught them how to swim.

In your wedding picture, you're so thin
thick hair piled in two wings.
His face is round, like my brothers.
In ten years he'll be dead
you and five children alone.

3

To me you were an Irish oak
transplanted in midwestern earth.

Who's afraid of Grandma Woulfe
we sang as children from the
wooden porch. *Who's afraid
of arms like branches, of fingers
working cotton and bread.
Who's afraid of wild gray hair.*

Feed your bones, you'd tell us.
Rest those tired bones.

4

I stand now where once you stood
beneath the fortress ruin,
sun held in its clear eye,
and I wonder about my bones.

What kind of bones are good?
And what are bad bones?
Ones that fold in upon themselves?
Ones that hide in flesh?
Were my bones formed
from those same genes
that made you strong?
Does that, will that make them good?

Your hands crocheted until you lost your eyes.
Your wedding ring is tight on my smallest finger.

The Ancient Order of Hibernians

My father was the oldest son.
He didn't have to wait to marry
the way they did in Ireland,
no land to gain, yet he waited.

When he was young he was wild.
From the third floor apartment
behind the Chatterbox Bar he roamed
Cathedral Hill and the spired city below,
a swinger of the twenties.
One New Year's Eve he slid down
the bannister of the St. Paul Hotel
and all over the city
eighty-year-old women
remember him and smile.

My mother's mother was treasurer
for the Ancient Order.
My father's mother needed to buy insurance.
So my father brought the payment
from his parents' apartment
down to the tall house, already old
off Rice Street, a block from the railroad
shops where my uncles worked.

Mother from behind lace curtains
watched him climb the wooden steps
a bespeckled Harry Truman in his thirties.
Since she was twelve she'd been working
without love. She ran to meet him knowing
                    it was time.

Reading the River

The rainbow above betrayed the squall which drove me
scuttling for shelter under the river bluff where the heron
stood fishing for minnows in the crevices and shallows.

In disgust or joy it cried a hoarse broagh, a low tattoo
among the ferns and wild rhubarb, ending suddenly
reminding me of the last consonants of Mrs. Connolly's words
as she bragged eternally about her sons—Mike, Tom, Sean,
and Pat who would be a Jesuit, while we stared at the ground.

My brothers and I needed words with heft and weight.
At Candlemas holy beeswax crossed in front of our clenched
adam's apples brought forth no language.
Our five pairs of hungry eyes rummaged through gleanings
and leavings on the riverbottoms. We searched the streets
of St. Paul. In the sluice-rush of our minds we waded
through backwash, mud and library books looking
for our stories, for the spillage, for the words
drizzling like seeds from the river cottonwoods.
Words, lost to our parents before us.

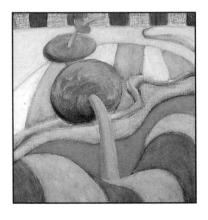

No Straight Lines

I go with my parents and my children
to the West Seventh Street parade.
The sunlight dances off the tops of oil tanks.
In the glaring light, senior citizens march,
many wheeling their own chairs.
No straight lines here. Some wave,
some hold beer glasses in one hand.

After them, the Knights of Columbus,
those serious-faced plumed fantasies
from my childhood, long swords glinting.

> *The dark church, those swords*
> *arched above departing caskets.*

Behind their measured steps, roar
the bikes from Harley Davidson.
Driven by grizzled faces,
fat bodies from the fifties.
Bikes spill across the pavement.

> *Big Dave in his T-shirt*
> *roaring over our front lawn.*
> *My mother worrying at the window.*
> *I would like to be one of those women riding*
> *alone in a halter top, long braid down my back.*

Today my mother laughs, so happy to be here.
"What kind of parade is this?" my older son asks.
He's missing the baton twirlers, the trained dogs,
the high school band we have at home, all marching
in place in the middle of the street.

> *"This is a West Seventh Street parade,*
> *This is where I grew up,"* I tell him.
The doors to all the bars are open.

Whose Hands Are These?

The onyx bay gives back those years
when my boys, up early, chose cereal
in small packages to eat on the beach.
Up at five, I sat on the dock
to watch sunfish breakfast on moths.

The sun first edges the island
in light, then spreads toward my shore.

When my sons took the boat alone
I listened for their motor, eyes
pleading with the blackening channel.

My twisting hands became my mother's hands.
She braided her fingers in worry even
as she was dying, waiting for her sons
to return one last time.

As I thought about calling the sheriff
the night became knife-edged.
Then the boat entered the channel
and the bay, the moon, the loon cry
were given back to me.

Behind me in the woods an owl lifts
from a tree too small to hold it.
I see its shadow first
then I freeze in an old dream,
wrapped in dark feathers
a soft conspiracy.

> Sail above me
> owl
> each moment now
> is yours

and I run
like your small prey
through chaos
the almost pattern of things.

Choose Me, Father

In church we learned that god
was like you so god for me was silent

a landscape of white snow and the moon
a shuffling off in the presence of language,
asking everything for nothing.

Stop over, you say now,
trying on words like a new suit.

They're too big, your voice loud.
Your hands get in the way.
Sometimes you give up in mid-sentence.

Christmas again and I take you to lunch.
We spend it talking about my mother
how she sent hundreds of cards, presents

for everyone. She talked for you then.
She was your insistent voice.

Who would have thought she'd be gone.
*I don't send cards. I haven't seen
the old neighbors since her funeral.*

Choose me, you say to me now. Choose
me for a few minutes a week and I do.
Better to talk to a father at fifty

than never. Better to take
a close look at your words, quaking
messengers from a distant kingdom.

Without Her, Nothing

⁀

In the mornings my father rose early
to shovel coal and fire the furnace
until the house shook with its roar.

I remember the glimpse of my mother's
pear breasts drooping over her stomach
as she dressed behind a chair by the vent.

I looked away embarrassed by so much
white flesh, afraid for my own thin body.

⁀

When my children surprise me dressing
I cringe at the flash of this memory.
My body's become like my mother's,
a soft runaway.

⁀

Before she goes, I will thank her —
my body — there for me
all of the time.
She stands in lines for me, sits
at a desk when she wants to run.
Eats what I give her.
Wears leather on her feet.
Duck feathers on her hands.

For years I put her in front of mirrors,
to catalogue her imperfections.
Never said, *you are lovely,* or looked
long into her eyes. Never let her enjoy
a touch or a man's words, *you have
a gorgeous body.* I'd whisper, *It's a lie.*

For all this, Body,
forgive me.
I'll find a softer place.
You stand tall
while I crouch inside.
You make love
for me who am still afraid.

Boatyard Late October

Plastic wrapped canvas shrouded
empty hulls of yachts and runabouts
beached on trailers
strewn all over the dusty lot.
We come last each year
pulling the smallest boat,
hoarding this heavy piece of summer
in the garage as long as possible.
It still echoes our noisy lovemaking
and the hollow slap of waves.
All summer we skimmed by yachts
waved to catamarans.
Here it rests beside a cabin cruiser
an equal in emptiness and no longer
prophetic against a sun-washed horizon
naming all rooted life incidental.

Around us autumn fields burn
a low chocolate before rotting brown.
Burled trees support acres of unbroken sky
and I wish for the dark boats
moving slowly in the night
want back the light barges
gliding silently to nowhere.
Wish for the docks in summer
places where what can't happen happens
where decisions are strung out
in the fine air between leaving and staying.

When I walk uphill toward home
part of me stays on the shore
fallen into the possibilities of going.
Like my Celtic grandmothers
I wait always for boats to return
dragging green promises, never kept.

Storyteller

(for Scott Kephart)

In October pumpkins line the wall.
Men in baseball hats replace the roof,
urgent bodies stark against the sky.
Snow on the way, one shouts,
hurry but hang on.

Those past Halloweens six pumpkins watched,
surprised o's for eyes as we told the children
ghost tales round the fire in the hills above the river.
Smile when you're afraid, we told them,
and ghosts will stop to count your teeth.

We worked all day to prepare, Shelby said,
*drew faces to carve, made props for stories
my dad would tell.*

One year Scott told the story of "Tailey Po"
lay on the ground and moaned while children
stole his stuffed sock tail.
Who has taken my Tailie Po?
Give me back my Tailie Po!

Scott was always the last to leave.
The rest felt the cold break of midnight air
while he still smiled at the sinking coals.
When a flame turns blue
it's a ghost passing through.

Scott died in October. With these stories
we try to cover the holes of loss,
those of us left standing on
this world's wild steep pitch.

III

HAUNTED BY THE THROBBING AND
THE WAY IT SHAPES TIME

January

Those black husks scattered
beneath the trees are shed skins
of autumn's cicada.
Don't clap yet.
It's a caesura.

February

The wind screams
I have news for you:

nests fall
cattails break
their shape is lost
cold seizes the bird wing
inside the earth
the cicada waits

That is my news.

March

It has nothing to do with age.
It's being willing to live in a beat
defined by its own tattoo.
Take your unsweatered body
outside. Do a wild dance.
Let the broken fingers
cicada
unclasp your skin.

April

My life unravels backward.
Each day's words have already been said.
On one poplar branch a cardinal
and a red-winged blackbird sing,
voices the same cicada
never close enough to have to break.

May

Through the school window
I see the curves of bridge
and planes. A swollen river snakes.
Smokestacks from the power plant
in the layered air. Spring in St. Paul,
old city still growing.
Through the hum of traffic, through glass
the voice of the cicada—urgent, relentless
orders me home.

June

Listen closely
to the swarming of bees
in the hibiscus.
A migration of cicada
have left their shells
like mummy cases on the trees.
Hear them buried but throbbing
beneath the ruins
cicada
cicada
cicada . . .
then thunder.

July

Cicada a sting
of sound never trapped
in the ground
its noise scrapes high
across the dry
night air a dull
blade needing repair

August

Metronome of summers
an aural abacus of days
that shimmer and disappear.
Or is it space that they enclose
another time which passes
on the song of the last cicada?

September

A gift of time
Who can give this
thing I thought I could count on?
My bedroom clock says nine
The paper says it's eight.
My watch still runs on Irish time.
For me it's six or seven
or no time but
light breaking from the rotting cells of leaves.
My husband walks naked after running
sweat still rolls down his face a glorious
peel of the leafless morning.
Nothing that can be saved.
He steps into my room just in time
into the patient time of the cicada.

October

If it is true   as the Irish say
that cicadas are the souls
of dead poets crying out
the things they did not write
when they lived
I will pray to them:
Give me your voices
oh cicadas.
Your songs
grow thin
in the dry weeds
along the railroad tracks.

November

The robins left weeks ago
the pregnant black cat
hunts in the yellow foliage
her belly brushes fallen leaves
a few cicadas sing.

December

What was the old monk looking for?
He left the monastery,
wandered through the twisted streets
of Dublin, eluding the young monks.
In the rain, up Grafton Street
he ran to Stephen's Green.

In front of Newman Hall
he stopped a black-robed nun.
"Help me, Sister," he said.
"I'm John the Baptist looking
for cicadas and wild honey."
"Come with me, prophet," she said.
"You don't even have to be good.
Get your knees off the ground
and shed that hair shirt.
Your time in the desert is over."

Coda

What if the trip is circular
like the rounded empty foot of the ladyslipper
we almost missed as we walked the old railroad bed
through the woods in the middle of our life together?

What if we return always to what was there
but we had to find, the same circle,
with a jut upward the makes a spiral?

The slipper was made for a storied foot,
a white moccasin stained with blood
an Ojibwe maid lost in deep snow,
continued barefoot carrying medicine.

It was made for a young heart which
sheds irony. I called you back to see
and you loved me for it.

Say the body is not on a conveyor belt
but is spiraling outward like the universe.
Say the flower is a sign for our journey

        that keeps us going, a
        reminder of other feet,
        a red-stained ticket.

IV

NEW HOMES, NEW PLACES TO DIE

Beneath Me, Behind Me

If these maple leaves fell upward
If the click of each spiraling
one and one and one
surrounded by its own silence
reversed
If gravity stopped for one moment
just here
then the leaves I lie on
would fly away like orioles
threading the evergreens
would take the migration path
like castro falcons

We study the blue sky
as if we were searching
for one thing, something simple
what is left
the real maple

but it's not like that

the loss is real
We walk deep in the red carnage
lifting leaves to the light
this thing that falls

Sing

I climb until my lungs hurt
glisten with sweat
see my arms grow bony.
Climb until I'm surrounded by peaks
stacked against the sky.
Stand at the edge of trees
near a lake hung with water lilies,
their pads upended by wind.

> *There is a voice here,*
> *call it my own,*
> *a voice telling me to sing*
> *for myself on this earth*
> *for the slim girl I was*
> *holding underwear full of blood*
> *for arms that held babies*
> *for a body that's changing*
> *rounded and safe like a hive*
> *to sing for brain, bone, skin*
> *for rain, stone, wing*

I remember the way my mother
dying told a life too late
the words I called gibberish
evaporating with a sigh the way
crickets are a circle of sound
a ring in the pool of night
that expands and ends in silence.

Her Hoof, Her Black Muzzle

I am biking on the concrete road,
eyes on pavement, mind searching
                for a word.
Air cool as it has been for days.
Sky constantly changing.
I hear before I see the deer.
A startled golden streak threads
the hardwood, the foliage veil.
She stops and turns to stare
at me across her oily back.
I stand on the road and look.
We watch each other a long time.
Her eyes don't blink, her leaf
                ears stand.

> *There is no other gold like that.*
> *She is much more beautiful than I.*

Suddenly she shrugs and walks
deeper in the trees.
I want to follow her into
the trembling mystery of green
stay to lose my color
when winter comes.
I bike home having forgotten
the word I wanted, the reason
I was searching.

> *What will I do with what's left*
> *of my life*
> *What in this world will I do?*

Paper Landscape

Palest wash of sun-bleached ink,
the mountain loses itself in dreaming.
Miniature thatched roofs blossom
on the valley floor, a place for the eye
to stay, leave, revisit, needing comfort.
A woman's hands cut paper, then inked it,
each tiny landscape different, sold
in a silk-covered box, bought by my son
in China, a gift on his return. How do
we bear this guessing at lives across
the dark? How do we lose the gaze
that sees but doesn't penetrate?
The woman bends over her paintings
her sleeves pushed back, her brush
strokes a feathered mist across water.
The paper a window for her, for us
as we follow her hand not knowing
the ones we meet or come home to.

Ceremony of Water

This end was buried in the sand
at the riverford where I hunted
rocks with Andy. I was brave then
as a water strider hunched on a lily pad.

In one great stride I leapt
with Andy holding my hand
skimmed the water's sweet face
over stones like black molars
over the shifty gaze of red agates
tourmaline of the heron's blue.

Moon they called me
and him the moon's child
all legs like the strider
all arms to hold on.

That and Not

In two hours the fog-bound night heron
has not moved from the neighbor's roof
snake neck and beak stretched
as if fishing in air
each mottled feather visible
on a tweedy breast facing north.

Could be a kind of goodbye
the same as I feel these days
over advancing bands of flame and fade.
Could be blessing the house
where a young couple wait
for a child to arrive.

Could be trying to see its own brightness
the way a mother studies her child
the angel's awed-by-her-beauty look
in Donatello's Annunciation,
all surprised tenderness that virgin.

Could be wanting a message
like the call from my son in L.A.
After filming a birth he wants to thank me
for having him, calls me a perfect parent
but I know the failures, I count them
leaf by plunging leaf.

This is a country where the cold wind
sends birds hurling themselves over lakes
in long strings of sentences.
The heron has waited too long.
Stay, risk the cold, I want to say
but I can't promise anything, not even
attention enough
to keep the gray body from lifting
into a sky, suddenly bereft.

Michaelangelo saw the end of it
Carved that pain into the mother's face

.

Letter From the Middle

I miss you most at harvest
when lake and sky join,
an uncertain line while wasps invade

the house seeking food and warmth.
Finding neither racoons grow bold.
Rummage trash cans

parade like gourmands across the roads.
Everyone buys chimney plates.
A cold friend from Texas wears down.

Northern lights feather the sky
with ragged blue and purple wings.
The heron is only a memory.

At my feet Superior nuzzles,
laps its broken shore. A mouse stretches
its neck, then scrunches into a tunnel

beneath the rocks while I face north begging
for a gift in the middle of my life
to keep me grounded when my body

wants to fly or burrow.

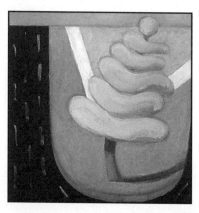

Her Winter Heart

1

When she lives in the north alone
she watches the black shape,
the limbus at the edge of the woods,
is glad when it slides into the moon
limned yard, sending the dogs
into paroxysms of barking,
filling the air like warnings
that shred her mind when an old fear
shifts and stirs.
She wakes to look for the bear
through leafless oaks
sees the lake lit with the still
clarity it gets just before freezing.
She finds her eating the last
apples, fighting against sleep.

2

Her winter heart is a mirrored lake
where clouds, water glide together
in a curtain of gray silk tinged with a pink
liqueur of wild berries.
A fog of frost smoke detaches from her heart
drifts from her mouth into punishing air.
Up and out of the dark the cold pulls
a garden of crystals.

3

When she lives in the north alone
a sea of snow rolls over the city
a few figures struggle to the liquor store
a snowmobile, a plow in the dark.
Marooned in an old house
she wears a path to the window
thinking of the bear that rolled
in from the woods each night
to sit in the sandbox next door.

In the morning between winds
she sees a gray sludge, a hole where
there were rocks and beaches
hears but cannot see
Superior, feels the emptiness
wants to leave town even though
nothing with wheels is moving.

She searches for the bear, remembering
how she'd watched her roll down the road
on round haunches. She knows they both
will wake with lust some morning
will walk on the ice with feet of fire.

Going In

Dismantle what
    the heart knows
Redefine this morning
    so it will be morning

Break through days
    into day
marriage into marriage
    into marriage
Wade into it deeper
    mouth deep

Unlearn perfection
Unlearn romance
Unlearn the sentence
to hear each word
the constellations
to see the stars

It's not going back
It's a new landscape
The old tracks washed away
the river ahead
    unwinds
    winds
Eat through wildness
    in that sweet body
to get to the body inside
    that body
you think you know

Advent

even if she is unknown by that perfect barn
off the freeway between North Branch
and Hinckley a scraped white leaning
slightly to the right with the sun rising
across from it nothing to stop it
finding the pink deep in the weathered wood
she knows barns endure

that something waits inside them for spring
even if she is a woman who watches
for doors to open, the ground to swell
for something to turn like the engine
of a tractor hidden but there even if
she waits for what grows

birth or death knowing Mary was a child
but Elizabeth was old and pregnant even
if it's all submarining beneath
the skin the earth the wood the metal
planning a savage valediction

even if from these bodies light pours

Neither Bones Nor Wings

It's not like the surf
but the soughing beneath it
a cello murmur

which is like not water on sand
in the morning heat but the sigh
of the sea rising from shells

music?
the memory of music?
Bach and water on stones?

I saw a woman at the river.
She was watching a night heron feed.
Her white arms could have been bones
or wings, a spatter of flesh.

A light shone around her,
from her.
Not spirit, not matter.

Camouflage

Egret walks the river bank,
eases toward the water,
eyes fixed on something moving,

darts, nibbles, winds
her serpent neck and cleans
feathers that radiate a scent

of white. All layers, patterns,
shading invisible to my eyes.

Like her, I glean and gather
all that lies before me,
even my decline.

I swivel my head,
missing the spot behind,
where my ending waits.

One morning will I touch
my face and find it smooth
as river rock,
no eyes to see?

Eye Cantos

In great silence

egrets
     squalling ibis
fluvial white swirl
     knock and natter
     mumble mutter

then silence
     a spreading attention

overhead an osprey flies, whistling
and hundreds of white necks
     lift in a frieze
     of fear

When we were young in the tiled cloister
we were stricken rigid like that sometimes
eyes on our god

Facing it

Loon, a foghorn in the bay
     bald eagle watches from an oak

Loon will not stop warning
     its baby swims behind the island

Eagle has babies too
     I've heard them in the nest
     above County 66

Keep custody of your eyes
the nuns told us, keep them low
don't see the enemy

We study

As I hike down from the mountain I find
        big horn sheep no longer fighting, rutting
        but full of love and hungry

I gaze long into the eyes of the leader,
        watchful with his raised,
        keratin-ringed head

Around us rivers plunge west and east

The nuns said, look inward
everything you need is there
we thought we'd find god hidden
in our stomachs, in our feet

Fertile dreams

My parents climbed a ladder
my mother, behind
to catch my father
when he fell,
but she fell before him
I've been dreaming them
the ones who have gone
in front of me, behind me

We stand
        at a great divide
keeping the other
        within eye reach

Symbiosis

There are spaces in old trees
          that open   into other lives
spotted choral orchids
          live on fungi at their roots
almost
but not quite parasitic   after flowering
         their tiny capsules nod.

Is it like that in me?   almost benign?
And how does the seeing affect it?
In the way a partial eclipse is seen as blood on the moon?

After fifty years bark buries fire scars in old trees.
The shape I see in my breast during the ultra sound
looks like basalt, eroded in the center,
a place for something to settle. I remember
my mother's scarred body, burns still raw
when cancer killed her. I turn away from both pictures,

think of the coniferous forest
         wolf lichen covers every trunk
cones hang
         like long fingers from the sugar pine,
soft   insides like flesh
         a deepest scarlet.

At the Blues Saloon

Dark in here . . .
walls painted black, lights low . . .
Frankie Lee works the crowd like a tent preacher
                Get hot! he shouts *Party!*
Dancers loosen their hips, arms become wings.
Bodies collide, sweat pours and the acoustics throb.
                Do ya feel good? Frankie wails
                Good! we shout back
                How do ya feel?
                We feel good!
saved again by an old singer, an old song . . .

      During the break I stand in the sound booth
      where a window opens to the sky
      framing, as if it were a painting,
      the big dipper where the north star points
      the way though a silence we know nothing of.
      I like the dark for what is shining.
      Silence for the sounds that shatter it.
      The space between sounds, between thoughts,
      where the spirit lives framed like the dipper,
      a finger points north to dark I don't want to travel . . .

Next on stage is old James Carr who croons.
On the floor each body melts into another.
I wrap my hands around your neck . . .

      First I'm called to a clearing by hundreds of birds.
      I stand in a circle of flutes all playing different tunes.
      Then you pull me back into the bush,
      into more than bush, everything angled, twisted
      swollen, torn, reversed, where roots split boulders, which
      crush ferns, water drips, gum congeals, lichen creeps . . .

Singer, take us down into dark
wavelike curl of the new frond
where life began, begins again
walls painted black, lights low . . .

Finding the Jungfrau

Balanced like moon and Venus, our roles switch.
When we set out to find the Jungfrau, I read the map.
We loved in sunflowers, those Old Men of the Mountain.
You were angry we missed Jungfrau, found another peak.
To me it didn't matter. I loved whatever we saw, named
but you seemed less accessible and yielding than stone.

In Western Ireland I took our son searching for stone
circles and hermits' beehive huts. Over switchbacks
we climbed finding ancient piles the books named.
I made him sit inside them, to find his heart's own map
then crawl out into rain-washed air, ready for peaks
away from me, in the distant mountains.

I wanted to be like Bridget on the mountaintop.
Now cornflowers remind me of campion spun from stone,
firmaments we saw on that not-Jungfrau peak.
Since that time our roles and minds have switched.
I must see the eight distinct petals marked like a map.
Today, of everything, I ask accurate and hefty names.

In a dream my shadow says the names
behind me as I walk downmountain.
It carries a bundle and chants a rhyme, a map
across silence: This burden is patient as stone,
soft to the touch, molecules of light that switch,
tenacious, restless as blooms at the peak.

Three steps from feathers to bone, Keats said at some peak
of vision. It's those steps I try so hard to name.
Today cows swing tails, sun turned to silver switches
around black bodies etched against the mountain
clumsy, love-full, as I am when I poise over you at some stoned
nub of pleasure, mind going with the body's other map.

In this weathering of spirit, this soul mapping
as erotic visions balance on their own gravelly peaks,
we find the Jungfrau, snowbound, crowned with stone.
You now want love and I want names on this
circuitous trail ravelling upmountain, where
keeping our balance, we've made another switch.

We, the mirrors as the mountain completes its naming.
Eros that blooms switches to roots, our winters mapped,
heat saved in stones gathered on sun-warmed peaks.

What can a woman take to keep the body open if the spirit closes, to keep the spirit open when the body closes?

Being old is just me being my own love
not an accumulation of years as I once thought,
not like the sediment layered in rocks,
but a rock itself loved by the tongues of the sea.

I won't live in a port without sea birds,
only the clang of departing ships,
on the pier, friends in dark coats
like magpies announcing a cold dawn.

I will write poems then to love myself by
to gentle the sharp-beaked bird.

Wildflowers will name the stories where I have loved:
hibiscus for the tropical city,
hedges of forsythia growing wild along mountain roads
and tended in island gardens,
small poppy fires in gray fields.

Yes I want a man in me, and myself in the mirror
listening to the dumb language of the tongue.
His tongue and mine moving from mouth to body,
finding new notes, new homes, new places to die.

Melody for a Long Marriage

The fins and backs of dolphins are like notes
sometimes tandem melodies, sometimes sequential
then a caesura   my arms continue

to keep the rhythm the way I learned to conduct
Gregorian chant in church, hands small cups
within the arms' wide waves, the sense of life

beneath as in the quiet words of Brancusi's sculptures
fish, swan, child in bronze, the spirit he glimpsed
as rounded essence, the leaping dolphin in us.

He caught the life I once dreamt: water boiling
beneath the surface, hot springs steaming
through an unstable country and yes
we could put our hands in that heat and we did.

Naming Them

(for Timothy at Cluny)

one woman sews, one looks in a mirror
one puts away her jewels

I think of you as I watch these children
sitting, legs crossed on the flagstone
of a museum once a monastery.
They're listening to stories the tapestries tell
the way you did that Sunday we came,
your ten-year-old mind hungry for history.
A poet reads to his lady
who holds a mirror to the face
of the unicorn surrounded by
thick burgundy and moss green
fruit-bearing trees, music from strings

We studied the Book of Hours, the planting scene
made beautiful by the monk's hands.
a flowery mead of daisy, cowslip, strawberry, viola.

You stopped at every portrait asking,
What did he do? Was he good or bad?
Together we hunted words, old names and times
lapiz   verdigres   Clothilde   Charlemagne

Grown, you returned on your own
like the young woman in the tapestry
a mon seul desir who turns from the past
after her own desire. Struck by a car

you were taken to the beautiful Hotel Dieu,
on the Place du Parvis Notre Dame.
Not beautiful inside you said and told
how you lay trembling with shock.
We are trying to find you a blanket but
at a public hospital in Paris, who knows . . .
the doctor shrugged. I never knew.
So much I do not, will not name.

Men still prune the vines wearing rust shirts
      forever women bend to loosen the earth.

Moorings

Looking for stones I see a heron lift off the shore
drift toward me and stand, her red eyes stones

still holding heat. This is the morning after
a dream of dying and not. A door banged in wind,

a white ship filled the harbor, but my old father
and I, stubborn as grass, refused to move toward that boat.

A muskrat swims knife straight, its nose in air.
Two fishermen pull their boat onto sand, pour coffee.

Its thick, I'm-still-alive smell tells me it's time to work.
Not now when I've stopped trying to outrace the turning earth.

I'm busy learning what I knew as a child on a bent road.

After My Father's Death

In Amsterdam airport I spend long hours
in lines bridged by time in the duty-free
among those repetitious objects of desire
perfumes, whiskey, ties mobs buy for *guilders*,
their languages comodified. Outside, airplanes arrive,
depart, snow falls and I think of you. Maybe your funeral
should have been here, this chaos a good place to leave.

You wanderd away from us suddenly, a nomad
having lived so long in one place, looking surprised
at what things had come. You refused our news,
the food you loved and followed your own way.

The priest mumbled your name, the saints' names,
"Pray for us," we answered numbed by ritual,
the strange incantations to Clotius & Fotius & all
those other men & two Marys, Magdalen and Mother.

And where are you now?
I'm not free of duty.
I carry your fragile bones
and will go where you have gone.

Snow falls on Amsterdam airport . . .
Snow is falling in St. Paul . . .
New snow piled like fresh laundry . . .
Old snow blowing over and over itself . . .

                    (After a poem by Adam Zagajewski)

81

Tall Birds Stalking

Stand in the lake of the ordinary
open to sky, to earth, to moon
be the bridge between sky and earth
like the great blue heron in the bay
light in the circle of her eye
rounding out the morning inside you.

Breathe in, breathe knowing
moments when you let wings
sweep your heart
sure as the rain song of a cello
the child playing in the sand
the young lover, the marriage
of three thousand nights
go in carrying, come out naked
knowing you are blest
that there's time to be
what you will be next
bird inside, outside you
filling your cracked, dry bowl.

Red Bird in Winter

I cannot keep you here with me.
You must live far off
but the human song of you
impregnates the day.
Helps me praise the beauty
of black limbs in new snow.
Above me the hill of shale
grows deeper with a pile
that won't be cut.

Where I live the northern edge
of water is absence of color
changing only in intensity.
When clouds of steam rise
from the cauldron of Superior
I turn to your memory for color.

The slivered moon hangs still
in the morning sings
against the end that sails
in on hollow light.
Because of this love
I'm like the piper you see
standing on sea's edge
who plays to the rising
southern sun not imitating hope
                    but creating it.

I dip my brush in the music
that tells me what we were
what I want to be. I hear
you sing through the wooly mist
and my heart, that hungry cardinal,
beats on in its cage of bone.

About the Author

Mary Kay Rummel's poetry book, *This Body She's Entered*, was chosen as a Minnesota Voices Award winner and published by New Rivers Press in 1989, and her poetry chapbook, *The Long Road Into North* was published by Juniper Press in 1998. Over the years she has had over 120 poems published in many literary journals and anthologies including Minnesota based publications such as *Loonfeather, Sidewalks, Minnesota Monthly, Minnesota Poetry Calendar, Artword Quarterly, Luna, Hamline Review, Great River Review, Sing Heavenly Muse* and others. Her poems have appeared in journals from other parts of the country including: *Nimrod, Bloomsbury Review, Alaska Quarterly Review, Passages North, Northeast, Flyway Literary Review, California Quarterly, Hawaii Review, Ibis Review,Primavera* and many others. She has also published work in Canada and Ireland.Recently her poems were included in the anthologies *The Talking of Hands* (New Rivers Press), and *Spud Songs* (Helicon Nine Editions). A short story appears in *Stillers Pond: New Fiction from the Upper Midwest* (New Rivers Press, 1991).

She received a Loft Mentor Award and residency fellowships to the Vermont Studio Center, May 1999, and for May 2000, and at Norcroft Retreat Center for Women, August,1999. She has given readings all over Minnesota.

Mary Kay Rummel has taught school and worked for the COMPAS Writers in the Schools Program and is now an associate professor of literacy education at the University of MN, Duluth.